THE
LOCKER
ROOM
PLAYBOOK

THE
LOCKER
ROOM
PLAYBOOK

A PRACTICAL GUIDE TO
Heal Hurt, Overcome Adversity, and Build Unity

DAMON WEST
Bestselling Coauthor of *The Coffee Bean*

STEPHEN MACKEY
Player Development Coach

WILEY

Published by John Wiley & Sons, Inc., Hoboken, New Jersey.
Published simultaneously in Canada.

For general information on our other products and services or for technical support, please contact our Customer Care Department within the United States at (800) 762-2974, outside the United States at (317) 572-3993 or fax (317) 572-4002.

Wiley also publishes its books in a variety of electronic formats. Some content that appears in print may not be available in electronic formats. For more information about Wiley products, visit our website at www.wiley.com.

Library of Congress Cataloging-in-Publication Data

Names: West, Damon, author. | Mackey, Stephen (Development coach), author.
Title: The locker room playbook : a practical guide to heal hurt, overcome adversity, and build unity / Damon West, Stephen Mackey.
Description: Hoboken, New Jersey : Wiley, [2023]
Identifiers: LCCN 2022015063 (print) | LCCN 2022015064 (ebook) | ISBN 9781119902683 (paperback) | ISBN 9781119902706 (adobe pdf) | ISBN 9781119902690 (epub)
Subjects: LCSH: Self-actualization (Psychology) | Equality. | Cancel culture. | Discrimination.
Classification: LCC BF637.S4 W4478 2023 (print) | LCC BF637.S4 (ebook) | DDC 158.1—dc23/eng/20220401
LC record available at https://lccn.loc.gov/2022015063
LC ebook record available at https://lccn.loc.gov/2022015064

COVER ART & DESIGN: PAUL McCARTHY

SKY10035752_092922

Contents

A Note from the Authors   *vii*

1 Eyes on the Prize   1

2 You're Better Than That   13

3 The Locker Room Is Broken   25

4 Growth Takes Place Outside of
   Comfort Zones   39

5 I Believe in You   53

6 Canceling the Cancel Culture   65

7 A Culture of Character   79

8 All In   91

9 The Six Pillars   103

10 In the Zone   115

11 Vulnerability Is a Strength   129

12 Team Meeting   141

13 Humility and Grace   153

14 I Want the Ball   165

A Note from the Authors

When we sat down to write *The Locker Room*, in the summer of 2021, we had one simple goal: to help people experience the "miracle of the Locker Room."

The "miracle of the Locker Room" is a concept where, on healthy teams, people from all different backgrounds, with all kinds of hurts, histories, and hang-ups, come together and agree to six concepts:

1. A common goal that is bigger than self.
2. Making a mistake doesn't make *you* a mistake.
3. Diversity is not an obstacle to overcome, but our strength to overcome our obstacles.
4. The standard is the standard.
5. Hard days, truths, and conversations are endured, received, and had.
6. The success of the team is greater than the success of the individual.

We believe that any time a group of people makes this commitment, whether in sports or life, the conditions are set for that team or organization to overcome adversity, heal hurt, build unity, and ultimately, reach their goals.

With *The Locker Room*, we wanted to tell the story of a fictional team as an encouragement and example to help you or your team or organization visualize the "miracle." Now, in *The Locker Room Playbook*, we want to equip you to experience the "miracle."

This playbook is designed for individuals and teams, and while it is simple, it won't be easy to get the most out of this playbook. It requires commitment, time, and vulnerability—and as we learned from Coach Smitty, "Authentic vulnerability is a strength."

Every chapter of the playbook mirrors a chapter in the book, and the chapters are separated into three sections: *For Everyone, For the Individual, and For the Team*. Let's look at how to use each section.

For Everyone

In the "For Everyone" section, we identify the core lessons from the chapter, summarize the chapter, and provide deep-dive-teaching information. While the first two segments are meant to serve as a refresher for what you read and learned, the deep-dive-teaching portion is designed to offer some "next-step thoughts" on how you can apply the lessons of that chapter to your life and team. These next-step thoughts are connected to the chapter, but go beyond what we could cover in the book.

For the Individual

In the second section, "For the Individual," we invite you to do some personal reflection and work to connect the lessons of the chapter to your own life. There is space for you to write your own key takeaways, plus some reflection questions based on the chapter and deep dive teaching, as well as an exercise that will help you turn your ideas into action.

For the Team

The final section, meant to be completed with other people, provides discussion questions and a group participation exercise for your team or organization. The questions have no "right" answers, only opportunities for you to share with each other, and listen to one another, in order to learn from the group. We believe that a team or organization can only reach their full potential when they listen to one another.

As with *The Locker Room*, our goal for *The Locker Room Playbook* is to help you experience the "miracle of the Locker Room." We believe that if you commit to bringing the best of you to the lessons in this playbook and to your teammates, you will experience just that.

With Humility and Grace,
Stephen Mackey and Damon West

1

Eyes on the Prize

For Everyone

Core Lessons

- There are subtle signs when a Locker Room is broken, but even the best coaches may miss those signs.
- The pressure to win should not be allowed to blind us to the needs of our team.

Chapter Summary

Coach Smitty is a well-respected coach with a winning team that could go all the way to a championship. But Coach Smitty has a problem: one of his star student-athletes has made racially offensive comments that were recorded and ended up on social media. Now everyone in the community and school is upset. Coach Smitty decides not to handle the matter in public, which causes further problems that he is not yet aware of.

Deep Dive Teaching

In the story, Davey is not held to the same standard as his peers. The problems with this are pretty obvious from our armchairs, but what about when we're faced with such a situation in the real world?

In reality, it can be all too easy to take the route that Coach Smitty did by relaxing the standard for the sake of a win. In this example, both Coach Smitty and Davey have allowed talent to outstrip character.

The Standard Is the Standard The standard exists as a benchmark. Not everyone will have the same talent or skill level, but everyone can meet the same basic standards of integrity, fair play, and work ethic. These are zero-talent skills that every single person on the team can develop.

But the standard only matters if everyone is held to it equally. If the standard is one thing for the star quarterback and another for the water boy, then it's not really a standard at all. No matter who violates the team code, the standard must remain the standard.

Talent Cannot Be Allowed to Outstrip Character Of the most successful people, the ones who make the greatest impact on their teammates and the world at large aren't necessarily the most talented. Instead, they are the ones who have the greatest character. Talent sets the floor, but character creates the ceiling. Or put another way, talent gets you in the door, but character determines how long you're welcome to stay.

When we place more emphasis on talent than character, it creates problems such as teammates held to unequal standards or "smaller" contributions to the team being discounted. The most talented players must be held to the same standard as the least talented players. When talent outstrips character, the entire team pays the price in a lack of unity and trust.

For the Individual

My Key Takeaways

1. _____

2. _____

3. _____

Journal Questions

1. What signs have you missed that may indicate something is wrong with the culture of your team or family?
2. How would you have handled the Davey issue?
3. What similar crises have you had to handle in your life?
4. How can you work to be more aware of problems simmering beneath the surface?
5. Have you ever made racist comments? How did the response to the jokes or comments make it seem like an okay or not okay thing to say?

Exercise

Be a Journalist for a Day

- Bring a notepad and pencil to practice.
- Write down as many details as you can about the people, the location, and what you actually do.
- Think about what details you would give if you were going to explain this locker room and practice setting to someone else.
- Look beyond the big picture to find the unique minor details about the people and location that would bring it to life in a newspaper or magazine article.
- Ask Who? What? Why? Where? and How? questions to help you see beyond what you *expect* to see, so that you can appreciate what is really there.

For the Team

Discussion Questions

1. What can go wrong if you focus too much on winning?
2. What are some signs that winning has become too important to the team?
3. Why is it important to balance goals so that winning isn't the only focus?

4. What is broken about your Locker Room? What are the indications?

5. Are you willing to work together to fix what's broken?

Exercise

Agree/Disagree Circle

- Have the group stand in a circle around some central point.
- Read the list of words and phrases included here one at a time (include or substitute your own words, too!). If a team member believes that the word or phrase is more important than winning, they step to the center. If they believe it is *not* more important than winning, they take a step backward.
- After each word or phrase, have one person explain why it is more important than winning and/or why it isn't more important than winning. Then have everyone return to the original circle.
- The goal is not for everyone to agree initially. The goal is to see where there are differences of opinion, so the team can have a discussion about priorities.

Selected Terms

Respect

Loyalty

Friendship

Individual achievement

Video games

Family time

Trophies

Character

Teamwork

Physical fitness

Mental health

Prejudice

Fishing/hunting

Homework/studying

Politeness/courtesy

Being tired

Being hungry

Losing a loved one

Integrity

Anger

Notes

_____

_____

_____

_____

_____

_____

_____

_____

_____

_____

_____

_____

_____

_____

_____

_____

_____

_____

_____

_____

_____

_____
_____
_____
_____
_____
_____
_____
_____
_____
_____
_____
_____
_____
_____
_____
_____
_____
_____
_____
_____

_____

_____

_____

_____

_____

_____

_____

_____

_____

_____

_____

_____

_____

_____

_____

_____

_____

_____

_____

_____

2

You're Better Than That

For Everyone

Core Lessons

- Friends don't let friends make mistakes without speaking up about it.
- Leaders have a responsibility to use their power and position to lift others up, not put them down.

Chapter Summary

Coach Washington is the team's Offensive Coordinator, but more important, he is Coach Smitty's friend. When Coach Washington sees his friend, a coach and leader, using his position and power to put down a player instead of lifting him up, he knows that he has to step in and say something. Because Coach Washington is Coach Smitty's friend, he can't just sit back and do nothing. He chooses the harder right over the easier wrong and pulls his friend aside for a private talk.

Deep Dive Teaching

Coach Smitty is Coach Washington's head coach, but he is also his friend. It takes a lot of courage for a friend to call out another friend the way that Coach Washington does, especially when that friend is a leader you respect.

How friends interact with each other depends on their unique relationship. But there are some common themes among friendships that stand the test of time:

> *Friends SUPPORT EACH OTHER in good times and bad.* Support doesn't require you to agree with their decisions or to help them commit self-harm. Support requires you to be there and to offer the most appropriate kind of help that you can.
>
> *Friends TELL THE TRUTH, even if it hurts.* Friends don't lie to each other just to keep the peace or to make each other feel better. A friend is someone you can trust to give it to you straight, even if they are telling you things that you don't want to hear.
>
> *Friends RESPECT EACH OTHERS' feelings and emotions.* You may not fully understand why your friend is upset, but you should respect their feelings and then try to empathize and not downplay it.
>
> *Friends GIVE EACH OTHER the benefit of the best.* You've heard of giving each other the benefit of the doubt, but that's a negative approach. When we give each other the benefit of the best, we assume that our friend is coming from a positive place, even if they say a hurtful thing.

Perhaps the most important characteristic of friendships that last lies in that repeated phrase "each other." Friendship is a mutual relationship. It can't be all one-sided or it won't last.

How we treat our friends and how we are treated by them in return determines whether our friendship becomes something legendary, like the bond between Coach Smitty and Coach Washington, or something that we forget until the high school reunion.

For the Individual

My Key Takeaways

1. _____

2. _____

3. _____

Journal Questions

1. Who are the friends, teammates, or coworkers that you would do anything for?
2. How have you helped your friend(s) see an issue more clearly?
3. When has a friend had to help you see something more clearly?
4. How are you a leader? What does that mean for you?
5. What are some of your responsibilities as a leader?

Exercise

Script the Scene   Imagine one of your friends has let you down in some way and you want to talk to them about it.

Use the following guide to write a few sentences to script how you would begin a conversation to help heal the hurt caused by them letting you down.

- In one or two sentences say exactly how they let you down. Be as specific as you can about what happened and why it upset you. But also be very succinct. This is just to get the ball rolling.
- Give them an invitation to explain their behavior.

Example:

- Yesterday, I was disappointed when you didn't show up for the concert that we'd been planning on for the past two weeks. It hurt that you didn't want to spend time with me.
- I'd like to hear what happened that kept you from meeting me there. I was worried about you.

Be sure to write the script on paper: don't just to think about it.

Two things to keep in mind while writing your script:

1. People tend to shut down when we use accusatory language, particularly when we emphasize "you." Instead, try to lead with "I" or "we" statements.

2. Don't make it all about you. The point of conversations like this is to heal hurts in a friendship. The friendship is about both of you. Keep in mind that this is an invitation to talk about an issue and find a solution. It's not an attempt to make them repent and beg for forgiveness.

For the Team

Discussion Questions

1. What makes a good friend?
2. What can make it difficult to be a good friend?
3. What role does a friend play when someone makes a mistake?
4. How should a leader use their power and position?
5. What do you want to accomplish as a leader?

Exercise

The Talk

- Split the group into pairs for a bit of conversation role-playing.
- Each teammate will take turns having a difficult conversation with the other. The teammate who is listening will respond either positively or negatively to the discussion, and the first speaker will need to adapt accordingly.

- Use the following list (or make up your own) to start the conversation.
- Switch pairs every 5 to 10 minutes.

The goal is for the team members to experience both good and bad conversations about difficult subjects with a variety of people, to get them more comfortable with starting these conversations in the first place.

Conversation Topics

Your friend isn't treating their girlfriend/boyfriend well.

Your friend cheated on a test.

Your friend yelled at someone who didn't deserve it.

Your friend didn't show up when they said they would. They let you down.

Your friend has been making bad lifestyle choices, such as drinking/smoking on the weekend.

Your friend lied to you.

Your friend gossiped about you behind your back.

Your friend bullied someone else.

Your friend didn't do their share of the work for a project. But they still took the credit.

Your friend is using their power or position in a negative way.

Notes

_____

_____

_____

_____

_____

_____

_____

_____

_____

_____

_____

_____

_____

_____

_____

_____

_____

_____

_____

_____

_____

_____

_____

_____

_____

_____

_____

_____

_____

_____

_____

_____

_____

_____

_____

_____

_____

_____

_____

_____

_____

_____

_____

_____

_____

_____

_____

_____

_____

_____

_____

_____

_____

_____

_____

_____

_____

_____

_____

_____

_____

_____

_____

3

The Locker Room Is Broken

For Everyone

Core Lessons

- There are physical signs of racism, but sometimes we need someone else to show us what those signs look like.
- Racism will destroy a team if it is allowed to exist in the Locker Room.

Chapter Summary

Coach Washington takes Coach Smitty into the locker room and asks him what he sees. With some guidance, Coach Smitty realizes that the athletes have all racially segregated themselves within the locker room. This causes Coach Smitty to realize how poorly he handled the subject of Davey's inappropriate jokes. However, Coach Smitty doesn't yet understand the full extent of the problem of racism in the Locker Room.

Deep Dive Teaching

Like friendship, leadership is unique to the person who is in that role and to the team they are leading.

This chapter shows many different parts of leadership. Let's look at three of the most important:

1. *Vision*

When Coach Smitty speaks of the Six Pillars on the walls, what he's really talking about is his vision for the athletic program. Your leader's vision may be expressed as the five traits or the four rules or similar. For the Northwest Tigers of the story, their leader's vision is expressed as the six pillars: Tough People Win, Integrity Over Everything, Growth Follows Belief, Excellence Everywhere, Relentless Effort, Service Before Self.

A clear vision can help the team unite and give them direction. But it's just a starting place.

2. *Perception*

Sometimes even a clear vision written on the wall can be smudged or misaligned by competing goals, like an overwhelming desire to win. Coach Washington takes on a leadership role as he helps Coach Smitty perceive the locker room as it actually is. Coach Smitty's vision has been distorted by the hope of a championship, but Coach Washington is going to shine a light on a dark area so that Coach Smitty can see things clearly.

The ability to adapt to another point of view is important to leaders. If Coach Smitty was unwilling to see what Coach Washington had to show him, there would have been no light bulb moment.

3. *Correction*

Coach Smitty's reprimand of the freshman for missing the basket with his towel might look trivial at first, but it's actually an important correction for the player. One of the Six Pillars is Excellence Everywhere. "Everywhere" includes the locker room, and leaving your dirty towel on the floor for someone else to pick up is not showing excellence. It's a little thing, but Coach Smitty is trying to teach his athletes that the little things matter.

Coach Smitty also receives correction when he and Coach Washington discuss how to fix the broken Locker Room. Coach Smitty has become aware of the symptoms, but he doesn't yet understand the root of the problem. Through Coach Washington's correction, Coach Smitty can further alter his perception, return to his vision, and get the team back on track to being a team.

For the Individual

My Key Takeaways

1. _____

2. _____

3. _____

Journal Questions

1. What does your Locker Room look like?
2. What happens when you try to fix Monday's problem with Saturday's solution?
3. What six pillars would you choose to describe your character?
4. Are those the same pillars you would use to describe your team's values? Why or why not?
5. Do you think racism is impacting your team? Why or why not?

Exercise

Gaining a New Perspective

- As you go about your daily routine, deliberately change something about your routine in each setting.

- For example, you could change where you sit, what you order to drink, or who you talk to.
- After experiencing each change, write down anything new that you noticed by stepping out of your routine.

For the Team

Discussion Questions

1. How do teammates treat each other on your team?
2. How did you choose your closest friends on the team?
3. What makes your Locker Room unique?
4. Is that uniqueness a good thing or a bad thing? Why?
5. What would be some signs that your Locker Room is broken?

Exercise

Group Identity

- Designate each corner of a room as A, B, C, and D. (A court, field, or diamond works well for this, too.)
- Ask the team members which answer they identify with most in the following list (A, B, C, or D), or create your own.

- Instead of verbally replying, the team members should physically group themselves in each corner according to their answers. Don't give them time to think about it. Use a timer if necessary.
- After each question, have at least one representative from each group tell the team what makes them happy or proud to be in that group.
- The questions are not meant to be serious. They're meant to give team members a chance to see similarities with their teammates in a lighthearted way so they become open to the concept of looking for similarities in more serious ways.
- For the last question, ask: Which of the following do you identify with? Make one of the answers your team mascot (or however you typically refer to the team). This will bring everyone to the same corner to remind them that they're all on the same team.

Identity Choices

Which color do you identify with? A) Green B) Blue C) Orange D) Purple

Which beverage do you identify with? A) Water B) Soda C) Juice D) Milk

Which animal do you identify with? A) Cat B) Dog C) Horse D) Bird

Which room do you identify with? A) Bedroom B) Living room C) Garage D) Kitchen

Which subject do you identify with? A) Math B) Science C) History D) Art

Which activity do you identify with? A) Skiing B) Drawing C) Surfing D) Playing cards

Which article of clothing do you identify with? A) Jeans B) T-shirt C) Sweatpants D) Swimsuit

Which type of weather do you identify with? A) Sunny B) Windy C) Rainy D) Humid

Which mythical creature do you identify with? A) Dragon B) Elf C) Unicorn D) Phoenix

Which genre of movie do you identify with? A) Romance B) Action C) Sci-fi D) Comedy

Notes

_____

_____

_____

_____

_____

_____

_____

_____

_____

_____

_____

_____

_____

_____

_____

_____

_____

_____

_____

_____

4

Growth Takes Place Outside of Comfort Zones

For Everyone

Core Lessons

- When having a difficult conversation, strive to carefully consider the words that you use; be slow to anger and full of grace.
- Prejudice means looking down on another person or viewing them as "less than" due to differences such as skin color or economic level.
- Racism is based on the imbalance of power between one race and another. The wielding of that power to maintain the status quo is a racist action.
- Just because a person does or says something racist does not make them racist, nor does it even indicate that they had racist intent. Sometimes it's just ignorance.

Chapter Summary

Coach Smitty protests that there's no way that racism is the reason the Locker Room is broken. In the face of his friend's ignorance, Coach Washington prays: "Give me the words to speak; help me be slow to anger and full of grace." The two coaches have a discussion about the difference between racism and prejudice. Coach Washington explains that although Coach Smitty and Davey are not "racists," their actions were based in racism because of the way that they used their power and privilege.

Deep Dive Teaching #1: Growth Takes Place Outside of Comfort Zones

Too often we shy away from things that would benefit us because we are afraid. We're afraid to try new things because we don't want to fail. We're afraid to meet new people because we don't want to look stupid.

That fear is not unique to you. Everyone has these fears about failure and fitting in. Most people fear confrontation as well, particularly confrontation with friends or family members. These fears make it normal to want to remain in your comfort zone.

But if the fear of failure or the desire to avoid confrontation is allowed to control your actions, that does the world a disservice. If Coach Washington hadn't had the inner strength to step outside his comfort zone to have an honest and open conversation with his friend about a difficult subject, their team would continue to fall apart.

Growth isn't easy. Remember what growth spurts feel like? They're kind of painful and they leave these weird marks on your skin that never go away. For awhile after a growth spurt, it might not even feel like it's your body. But then you settle in, and what was new and unfamiliar becomes the comfort zone.

Growth takes place when our comfort zone becomes too small to serve our needs. No matter how afraid we might be of stepping outside the zone, it may help to know that we will grow into the new space. Someday, it will even feel comfortable again. At which point, naturally, it will be time to step out and grow again.

Deep Dive Teaching #2: You've Got to Know Your Anger Rights

Coach Washington briefly reminisces on the coach who taught him the "anger rights," but let's dive a little deeper into what those rights are.

1. *You have the right to be angry, but you don't have the right to be disrespectful.*

   Throwing a helmet on the ground due to anger is a sign of disrespect to your team on the bench and your family in the stands. Being rude or unfeeling due to anger is also a sign of disrespect to yourself and others. You have the right to be angry, but not if you allow that anger to drive you to disrespect yourself or your family.

2. *You have the right to have anger, but your anger doesn't have the right to have you.*

   Just like you have a responsibility to be a safe driver after getting your driver's license, you have a responsibility to be in control when you get angry. When you forfeit control of your anger, you forfeit the right to be angry. Anger is not responsible for your actions; you are.

3. *You have the right to get angry, but it's not right to get there too quickly.*

The more quickly you get angry, the more destructive it becomes. With a short fuse, you don't have time to reflect on how you can best respond to a situation. The more slowly you anger, the more perspective and information you gather, which you can use to help you manage your anger effectively.

Anger isn't any more inherently wrong than fire. But like fire, it can be destructive if it's not kept within boundaries. You have certain rights when it comes to your anger, but those rights can be forfeited if you let your anger control you instead of the other way around.

For the Individual

My Key Takeaways

1. _____

2. _____

3. _____

Journal Questions

1. What is your definition of racism?
2. What experiences have led you to that definition?
3. What privileges do you have? What privileges do you think others have that you don't?
4. What does it feel like to wield your power? And how does it feel when someone else wields their power over you?
5. Look back on Coach Smitty's initial reaction to hearing that racism is why the Locker Room is broken. How much do you agree or disagree with his reasoning? Why?

Exercise

Wisdom, Control, and Grace

- Create physical reminders for yourself to choose your words wisely, control your anger, and give grace to others.
- These reminders could be strips of paper with the prayer written on it that you tuck in your pockets or into your books or your wallet.
- If you're more crafty, create a model, paint a picture, or write a song that will serve as a reminder.

Following are some alternate phrases that can be used. Find what you connect with among these or create your own versions. The meaning is more important than the message.

- *Wisdom*: Give me the words to speak. Help me choose my words with care. Let me consider the impact of my words on other people. Words matter.
- *Control*: Help me be slow to anger. Give me a calm, peaceful mind. Let my anger only come out when it is useful to others. Remember the "anger rights."
- *Grace*: Help me to be full of grace. Let me give grace to those who deserve it least. Help me to release my anger in favor of grace. Give me a grateful heart and grace-full compassion.

For the Team

Discussion Questions

1. What are some hurtful or accusatory phrases that you should avoid when talking about racism? What are some alternative phrases that you can use instead?
2. Why is it important to be slow to anger and full of grace when talking about difficult subjects like racism?
3. How has racism (an imbalance of power based on race) affected your team?

4. What is the difference between being a racist and doing something that is racist? Why do these differences matter?

5. How would you recognize prejudice or racism? What are some examples of what those two things (individually or together) look like?

Exercise

Powerball

Follow these steps:

1. Divide the group into two equal teams (A and B).

2. Team A gets 10 dodgeballs at the mid-court line. Team B stands around one of the hoops.

3. Team A has two options with each turn. They can either try to put the ball in the hoop or try to tag out one of the Team B members.

4. If Team A chooses to take a shot at the hoop, Team B will watch the shot. If it goes in, the ball goes back to Team A. If it doesn't go in, Team B can try to catch it before it stops bouncing (or hits a wall). If they catch it, that ball is no longer in play and one of the "out" players can come back in (see next step).

5. If Team A chooses to try to tag out one of Team B, it's just like dodgeball except with no catching. Team B can only try to dodge. If one of the players

on Team B is hit, Team A gets the ball back and the person who was tagged is "out." If they miss, the ball is no longer in play.

6. Play ends when either the balls are all out of play or there are no more members of Team B on the court. Alternatively, play can go for a predetermined amount of time, such as 5–10 minutes. After the first round, have players swap sides and run it again so everyone experiences both sides of the exercise.

Notes:

The purpose of this exercise is to expose team members to both sides of the power imbalance. Use the following points to facilitate a deeper discussion about racism, based on the analogy of the powerballs.

AFTER both teams have played each side of the court, explain or read the following:

- The balls represent power. In this scenario only some had the power, and the rest couldn't touch it. Think about what it felt like to have that power and what it felt like not to have it.
- How did those with the power use it? When aiming for the hoop, they used their power to achieve a goal that didn't hurt anyone. When aiming for the members of Team B, they used that power to put others down. Aiming for the hoop is normal and expected. Aiming for others is harmful and, in some circumstances, racist.

Notes

_____

_____

_____

_____

_____

_____

_____

_____

_____

_____

_____

_____

_____

_____

_____

_____

_____

_____

_____

_____

_____

_____
_____
_____
_____
_____
_____
_____
_____
_____
_____
_____
_____
_____
_____
_____
_____
_____
_____
_____
_____
_____
_____
_____

_____

_____

_____

_____

_____

_____

_____

_____

_____

_____

_____

_____

_____

_____

_____

_____

_____

_____

_____

_____

_____

_____

_____

5

I Believe in You

For Everyone

Core Lessons

- An eye for an eye will leave the whole world blind.
- Repay hate and hurt with humility and grace.

Chapter Summary

As they prepare to tackle the problem of the broken Locker Room, Coach Smitty asks Coach Washington why he isn't mad or resentful of him for the way he acted. Washington tells him about the day in his childhood when a local bully took things too far. After Washington (then only a boy) caught the bully yelling insults at his mother, Washington lost control and beat up the other boy. His mother was disappointed in him for resorting to violence, and the incident left a permanent mark. That day Washington determined that he would repay hate and hurt with humility and grace rather than more hate and hurt.

Deep Dive Teaching

If violence isn't the answer, then what is? Unfortunately, there's no one thing that will solve the issues of racism or bullying. But there are many tools at our disposal to chip away at the problems. Let's look at three important ones that were hinted at in the previous chapter when

Coach Washington prayed "Give me the words to speak; help me be slow to anger and full of grace."

Communication   The words that we use, as well as our tone and body language, help us to communicate with others. Whether that communication is effective depends on our intent, our message, how we deliver that message, and how the other person receives it. We can't control how the other person will receive or respond to what we say, but we can seek to communicate with the right intentions and think carefully about our words.

Self-Control   Offense is something that is given, but it can't be forced on us. Just because someone says or does something offensive does not mean we have to take offense. It's not ours; it's theirs. In other words, we can let it go. We can acknowledge how someone's words or actions make us feel without needing to respond in kind. We can be angry without having to express that anger right then and there.

Empathy   Giving grace becomes much easier when we empathize with the other person. Everyone has reasons for their actions, even if those reasons are well hidden or don't make sense to other people. Everyone has their own pain and difficulties, even if they hide them from the world.

Empathy helps us recognize this. You don't have to understand another person to empathize with them; you just have to recognize your shared humanity.

Violence isn't the answer to racism or bullying. Instead, meet racist or bullying actions with communication, self-control, and empathy.

For the Individual

My Key Takeaways

1. _____

2. _____

3. _____

Journal Questions

1. Have someone's words or actions ever pushed you past your limits of self-restraint?
2. What helps you maintain your calm when others are hateful or hurtful?
3. What is an example of when someone gave you grace? How can you share that grace with others?
4. What words or phrases from others can trigger your anger?
5. How can knowing these triggers help you keep from resorting to violence when you hear them?

Exercise

Mirror Mirror

- Make a list of words and phrases that make you want to react with violence.
- Stand in front of the mirror and say these things to yourself (with any appropriate context to make them full sentences).
- First, notice what it feels like to say them. Then, focus on how it feels to hear those things.
- Write down what you felt during the exercise. Be specific in naming the emotions and what they physically felt like. There are no right or wrong answers. Feelings are just feelings.

This exercise serves two purposes:

First, it helps you stand on both sides of the words, so you gain a broader perspective.

Second, describing your feelings is important in helping to manage emotions like anger or frustration.

For the Team

Discussion Questions

1. Why is violence a poor reaction to hateful or hurtful words?

2. What is a more effective response when someone is hateful?
3. How does humility help you to respond effectively rather than reacting poorly?
4. What are some reasons why it's good to give grace?
5. Does your team have a problem with violent words or actions? What can you do to help resolve that problem?

Exercise

Grace Statements and Requests

- Have each team member write down five Grace Statements or Grace Requests on individual strips of paper.
- *Grace Statements* are a single sentence that extends grace to a teammate or coach for something they've done.
- *Grace Requests* are a single sentence that requests grace from a teammate or coach for something the writer has done.
- Fold up the strips of paper and put them in a hat, helmet, or other receptacle.
- Team members will take turns drawing a Grace Statement/Request and reading it aloud. This provides a level of anonymity for the shy folks, and it gives everyone a chance to look at grace from new perspectives.

The statements and requests should be a mixture of silly and serious. Here are a few examples:

- Tim, I forgive you for eating Chipotle before coming to practice.
- Mark, please accept my grace for our argument last week. I hope you will extend the same to me.
- Jasmine, I forgive you for taking the last bag of Cheetos from the snack stash at the last match.
- Desiree, please give me grace for the thoughtless comments I made yesterday.
- Coach, I ask for your grace because I phoned it in during the last drill on Monday.

Notes

_____

_____

_____

_____

_____

_____

_____

_____

_____

_____

_____

_____

_____

_____

_____

_____

_____

_____

_____

_____

_____

_____

_____

_____

_____

_____

_____

_____

_____

_____

_____

_____

_____

_____

_____

_____

_____

_____

6

Canceling the Cancel Culture

For Everyone

Core Lessons

- You must know where you are before you can get to where you want to go.
- Having a tough conversation with others requires humility and grace.
- If you're grippin' you're trippin'. Let go of your pride, so you can listen.
- It's easy to "cancel" someone. It's hard to give them grace.

Chapter Summary

Coach Washington asks: Where are we? Together, Coach Washington and Coach Smitty determine that the only way to answer this question is to listen to the team. Coach Smitty worries that this will be a heated discussion, but they agree that as long as they show authentic vulnerability and lead with humility, things will be okay. Coach Smitty confesses that part of the reason he handled the situation so poorly was his fear that either he or Davey would be "canceled" as a result of Davey's actions. The coaches agree that the Cancel Culture hurts much more than it helps, as people are too quick to dismiss others and not quick enough to give grace.

Deep Dive Teaching

The Cancel Culture is about gripping onto hate and offense. Participants in the Cancel Culture grip tightly to the hurtful things that have been said or the harm that has been done, not to make things better for everyone but to make sure that others are hurt, too. The Cancel Culture says: you hurt me, so I'm going to write you off. But as we say in the locker room, if you're grippin' you're trippin'.

Imagine this situation. One day a monkey finds a banana that he can only get by reaching through a hole in a log. But he can't get his fist out of the log while gripping the banana. The monkey can't get his paw out because his instincts are telling him to hold onto the banana. We have similar instincts, but unlike the monkey, we have the mental flexibility to choose a different path.

We can choose to let go.

Everyone has things they hold onto too tightly at some point, such as pride, anger, or fear. Coach Smitty held too tightly to his pride, so he didn't hear what Marcellus was trying to say. Davey held too tightly to fear, which kept him from owning up to his mistake and demanding to be held to the standard.

When Coach Smitty lets go of his pride, he opens himself up to learning how to overcome the problems that his team faces. Gripping onto things like pride, fear, or hate doesn't do us any good. These things just hold us back from reaching our full potential.

Gripping onto things that hold you back will just leave you tripping over your own feet. That's why we say, if you're grippin' you're trippin'. It's true in the locker room and it's true in the wider world. Hanging onto hurts will leave you aiming to hurt others in turn, but releasing those hurts gives you room to grow away from the incident.

For the Individual

My Key Takeaways

1. _____

2. _____

3. _____

Journal Questions

1. How have you been impacted by the Cancel Culture?
2. How does pride prevent you from listening to others?
3. What are you gripping onto that would be better let go?
4. Where are you on the journey to understanding racism?
5. Why is it good or helpful to approach conversations with humility and grace?

Exercise

Here are three different ways that you can symbolically let go of something you've been gripping onto. These won't magically make you stop thinking about the mistake or the hurt or your pride. (Whatever you're thinking of for this exercise probably has a strong hold.) This is just a first step to letting go.

The Flush
- Write the thing you want to let go of on a piece of toilet paper.
- Flush it down the toilet.

The Burn
- Write the thing you want to let go of on a piece of notebook paper or newspaper.
- In a controlled environment, like a firepit or a grill, burn the piece of paper.

The Trash
- Write the thing you want to let go of on fancy paper or the inside of a card.
- Tear it to pieces and throw it away in the trash.

For the Team

Discussion Questions

1. Where is your team starting from on the issue of racism?

2. How can you practice listening to your teammates?

3. How can humility and grace help you to have better conversations about racism and other difficult subjects?

4. How has the Cancel Culture impacted your team?

5. What are you collectively gripping onto that prevents your team from succeeding?

Exercise

Canceled by the Judge-and-Juries   This exercise is for a group of 10–20 people. It is adapted from a popular party game known as "Mafia" or "Werewolf."

- Everyone sits in a circle (either in chairs or on the floor), with their eyes closed—except for the leader.
- The leader walks around the outside of the circle and announces the role they are giving out and then taps the chosen person on the head or shoulder. (Everyone's eyes remain closed during this part). The roles given out are:
  - Three Judge-and-Juries
  - Two Fact Checkers
  - One Hero

Once people are chosen, gameplay proceeds in two phases: Night and Day.
Night Phase

Directed by the leader, players take the following steps:

- Everyone's eyes remain closed.
- The leader directs the Judge-and-Juries (J&J) to open their eyes. Through silent gestures, the three agree on someone to be canceled. They close their eyes again once an agreement is reached.
- The leader next directs the two Fact Checkers to open their eyes. Together they choose a person (silent gestures again) who they think is a J&J. The leader confirms or denies, and the Fact Checkers close their eyes again.
- Finally, the leader directs the Hero to open his or her eyes. The Hero indicates one person that they want to save and closes their eyes again.

Day Phase

Directed by the leader, players take the following steps:

- Everyone opens their eyes and the leader explains who has been judged.
- The judged person speaks about why they shouldn't be exiled from the community. Then the rest of the group has a discussion, siding for or against the judged person, and votes on whether to keep the person in the group.

- If the person is voted out, they join the leader outside the circle and are able to see everything during the next Night phase, but they can't give any hints to the remaining players.
- If the person is voted to remain in, they get to pick who they think is one of the J&J players to be removed from the group (canceled).
- If the Hero chooses to save the person voted out, that player receives grace and no one is kicked out that round.

The game is over when all J&J players have been removed from the community or when only J&J players remain.

Notes

_____

_____

_____

_____

_____

_____

_____

_____

_____

_____

_____

_____

_____

_____

_____

_____

_____

_____

_____

_____

_____

_____

7

A Culture of Character

For Everyone

Core Lessons

- It's hard to lead if you've never been taught how to do it.
- Culture isn't created by one person; it takes a buy-in from the whole team.

Chapter Summary

While Coach Washington takes a break from the whiteboard, Coach Smitty contemplates the culture he has instilled in the football program at Northwest. That culture includes the Six Pillars, but it's much more than that. In response to the concerns of his athletes, Coach Smitty established the Northwest Leadership Academy to teach his students how to lead, and the players helped to come up with the Six Commitments that all Northwest football players must adhere to as a standard of behavior. Coach Smitty notes that the culture he tried so hard to build is working, because now it has called him to be accountable for his actions.

Deep Dive Teaching

While Coach Smitty was developing the culture of the football team, one of his student athletes was courageous enough to admit that he didn't know how to lead, because he'd never been taught. Here are three steps to help you learn how to lead:

1. *Listen*

    The first step to learning anything new is listening to people who have already done it (or at least something similar). This could be listening to a person you know in the real world, watching a video online, or reading a book.

2. *Learn*

    Learning is not a passive act of absorbing information. If it was, tests would be a lot easier and wouldn't require any studying. Learning is what happens after we listen carefully. Learning happens when you repeat the information to yourself in new ways or when you think of examples from your life for how the information might apply. To learn, you have to think.

3. *Lead*

    Thought must turn into action. The only way to really figure out how to be a leader is by leading others. Some things just have to be done to be fully learned. You can listen to those who have gone before you and learn what they have to teach by thinking about it deeply. But to truly be a leader, you have to lead. It's that simple and that difficult.

For the Individual

My Key Takeaways

1. _____

2. _____

3. _____

Journal Questions

1. If you were designing a team culture, what would it look like?
2. How would you get a buy-in from the team to support that culture?
3. What makes a person a leader?
4. Are you a leader? Why or why not?
5. Who holds you accountable for your actions?

Exercise

Leadership Emblem   Create an emblem to represent the type of leader that you want to be.

- If you aren't much for drawing, just draft out the ideas in words instead of sketching, but pick concrete imagery. For example, if courageous leadership is something you want to represent you, write "roaring lion" or "soldier" instead of simply "courage."

Additional examples are provided next.

Images as Emblems

Integrity: moose or scales of justice

Excellence: five stars or trophy

Purpose: arrow or bull's-eye

Perseverance: lotus or beaver

Patience: ox or owl

Loyalty: dog or heart

For the Team

Discussion Questions

1. What does it mean to have good character?
2. What does a culture of character look like for your team?
3. Why does character matter?
4. What do you want your teammates to hold you accountable to?
5. What makes a good leader?

Exercise

Who's It Gonna Be?

- Divide the team into small groups of three to four people.

- Each small group must come up with words to create a cultural acronym for your team or organization, like the Six T.I.G.E.R.S. Pillars. The first letter of each pillar is one of the letters in the word "TIGERS," which is the Northwest mascot. (Two additional examples follow.)
- You can use your mascot, your organization name, or a one-word phrase that's important to your team to create the representative acronym.
- After a set amount of time (10–15 minutes should be plenty), the groups will present their ideas. Gather the best and/or most popular ideas on the board and work together to pinpoint what set of words best fits the type of team culture you all want to have.

Cultural Acronyms

Earnest

Accountable

Gritty

Level-headed

Eager

Sage

Never give up

Open-hearted

Robust

Tough

Healthy

Warrior

Effort

Safe space

Trustworthy

Notes

_____

_____

_____

_____

_____

_____

_____

_____

_____

_____

_____

_____

_____

_____

_____

_____

_____

_____

_____

_____

_____

_____

_____

_____

_____

_____

_____

_____

_____

_____

_____

_____

_____

_____

_____

_____

_____

_____

_____

8

All In

For Everyone

Core Lessons

- Culture is a reflection of leadership.
- A team must be united by one vision.
- Everyone has different experiences in life, but as humans we can all empathize with each other.

Chapter Summary

Where do we want to be? Coach Smitty and Coach Washington discuss the importance of having a single, cohesive vision for the team. If the team is pulling in different directions, they won't get far. But if everyone is giving their best effort at what is right in front of them, they can do something crazy like pulling a defunct truck 100 yards. Although Coach Smitty has not experienced racism directed at him, he can still empathize with his friend, who has experienced racism firsthand.

Deep Dive Teaching

Champions go all in on their goals. They go all in on their team. Let's look at why that is and what can hold us back from going all in.

Why should we go all in?

When we go all in, we accept the vision that our team leader has put out there. When we go all in, we find the strength to overcome any obstacle. When we're all in on the vision, that means we're all in on the team.

This matters because we can't achieve our team goals if we're holding something back. By saving that little bit of energy, we aren't reaching our full potential in the moment. This in turn keeps us from moving forward. It's an anchor that holds us back from reaching our goals and dreams.

What holds us back from going all in?

Thoughts like this hold us back: What if I put all I have into this moment right here and it doesn't work out? What if I give it my all throughout the game, and then I'm stuck in overtime with no energy left?

"What if" is a mindset that strangles your ability to give your all to anything. When you focus too much on what could potentially happen, the fear of not being prepared for it can cripple you. You stop focusing on pouring your heart, soul, and sweat into the right now, and start worrying about saving a little for the maybe later.

It's only when we let go of the "What if" mindset that we can go all in on our goals and dreams. And it's only when we go all in on our goals that we are able to go all in on our team.

For the Individual

My Key Takeaways

1. _____

2. _____

3. _____

Journal Questions

1. What is your vision for your team?
2. Are you all in on your team? How so?
3. How does the vision impact the team culture?
4. When have you felt empathy for another person?
5. How did that empathy impact your feelings and actions toward them?

Exercise

Mind Mapping

- Think about your team's culture and vision. What words and phrases come to mind?
- In the center of a piece of paper, write one word or phrase that describes the team's culture. From there, draw lines and write other words that are connected to this central vision.
- Continue adding lines with relevant words until you fill the page.

Here is an example:

For the Team

Discussion Questions

1. What is the single, cohesive vision for your team?
2. Why is that the goal? Why does your team want to achieve that vision?
3. What does it look like when you go all in on your team?
4. How do you demonstrate empathy for your teammates?
5. Why is empathy an important skill for a good teammate?

Exercise

All In Tug-of-War

There are two stages to this.

First: separate the group into two teams holding either end of a long, sturdy rope with something attached to the center. The teams will try to pull the center marker to their side of the median (a line on the ground, a stick, a convenient rock, etc.) while the other team is trying to do the same, pulling in the opposite direction.

The first stage requires the team members to go all in to win.

Second: Tie a towing cable to a car or an ATV or a wagon loaded with concrete. Something heavy that's on wheels is what you want. The whole group must work together as one to pull the heavy weight a certain distance.

The second stage requires the team members to go all in together to achieve a single common goal.

Notes

_____

_____

_____

_____

_____

_____

_____

_____

_____

_____

_____

_____

_____

_____

_____

_____

_____

_____

_____

_____

_____

_____

_____

_____

_____

_____

_____

_____

_____

_____

_____

_____

_____

_____

_____

_____

_____

_____

_____

_____

_____

_____

_____

_____

_____

_____

_____

_____

_____

_____

_____

_____

_____

_____

_____

_____

_____

_____

_____

_____

9

The Six Pillars

For Everyone

Core Lessons

- A team's culture must be built of concepts that the whole team buys into.
- The specific concepts are less important than the team's agreement to abide by those concepts.
- To get from where you are to where you want to be, you have to stick to the team's stated culture.

Chapter Summary

Coach Smitty takes some time to go over the Six Pillars of his athletic team's culture. He has worked hard to instill these concepts as the pillars of the program, and now those Six Pillars are going to help him work through the racism problem that his team is facing. In previous chapters, Coach Smitty and Coach Washington discussed where they were and where they want to be. In this chapter, Coach Smitty lays out the concepts that are going to help them get there.

Deep Dive Teaching

The Six Pillars of the Northwest Tigers are good concepts to incorporate into just about any athletic program or team culture. But the pillars themselves are less important than what they represent. Let's look at what makes the pillars work so well.

Zero-Talent Skills   Each of the pillars represents a zero-talent skill. That's something that anyone can do regardless of their physical abilities. Everyone can give relentless effort even if they can't throw accurately farther than a yard. Everyone can cultivate toughness through hard work and grit, even if they flinch when a ball is kicked in their direction. Everyone can strive to be excellent in the little things, even if they struggle with the big things.

Focus on Character   The focus of each pillar has nothing to do with winning championships. Instead, the pillars are all about how to be a champion. A trophy doesn't make you a champion. Having more points than the other team at the end of the game doesn't make you a champion. Being a champion is about living with character every day of the week. Champions are only as good as their character.

Life Lessons   The Six Pillars were created by Coach Smitty to help his team win championships and to turn the athletes into champions. But what they really teach the athletes (and coaching staff) are life lessons. Each of the Six Pillars goes beyond the game. They apply to playing the sport, of course. But ultimately, toughness, integrity, growth, excellence, relentless effort, and service all go beyond the scope of a football game.

For the Individual

My Key Takeaways

1. _____

2. _____

3. _____

Journal Questions

1. Which of the Six Pillars is most important to you?
2. Which of these do you struggle with most in your life?
3. What six words or phrases would you choose to live by that require zero talent, focus on character, and teach life lessons?
4. How do you think the Six Pillars can help Coach Smitty's team overcome the issue of racism they're facing?
5. What are some other locker room or team issues that pillars like these can help a team face?

Exercise

Personal Pillars of Excellence

- Use the three columns below to create your personal pillars of excellence.
- Choose six truths about where you currently are in life or on the path to your goals. This is the reality of your situation
- For each of these truths, write what the end goal (the ideal) looks like.
- Finally, create a one- to three-word pillar to help you get from the reality to the ideal. An example is provided on the first lines of each column.
- Feel free to use as few or as many lines as needed to identify the pillars that will help you go from where you are to where you want to be.

Where I Am (Reality)	Where I Want to Be (Ideal)	How to Get There
Overweight and easily tired	Fit and able to take long hikes	Diligence = Best work

For the Team

Discussion Questions

1. Refer back to the cultural acronym you created in Chapter 7. What words or phrases did your team decide on?
2. How have you lived out those concepts since that discussion?
3. When have you had an opportunity to live out those concepts but have fallen short?
4. Which of the Six Pillars from this chapter resonated with you most?
5. How are your team's pillars or concepts similar or different from those in this book?

Exercise

Pillar Talk

- Lay out markers for each of the pillars your team agreed on in the Chapter 7 exercise. These could be chairs, Hula-Hoops, cones, or similar—just something to represent the six or so pillars of your team culture. These should be spread out over a good-sized distance, such as a basketball court or half a football field.
- Create a list of questions related to the pillars (some follow, provided for inspiration).

- When each question is asked, team members run from a central starting point to one of the pillars, based on their personal answer.

This exercise opens up the opportunity for deeper discussion about the importance of the pillars and how they apply both on the field and in the game of life.

Pillar Questions

Which pillar helps you succeed in class?

Which pillar helps you be a better athlete?

Which pillar do you understand the least?

Which pillar is your favorite?

Which pillar helps you be a better member of your family?

Which pillar helps you be a better teammate?

Which pillar is absolutely indispensable on the field and off?

Which pillar reminds you of something you've already learned?

Which pillar feels like completely new information?

Which pillar makes you want to tell other people about it?

Notes

_____

_____

_____

_____

_____

_____

_____

_____

_____

_____

_____

_____

_____

_____

_____

_____

_____

_____

_____

_____

10

In the Zone

For Everyone

Core Lessons

- Where you focus, you finish.
- Be a coffee bean.
- When you mess up, make your apology proportional to the mistake.
- No one is above the standard.

Chapter Summary

Coach Smitty and Coach Washington discuss the practical next steps to put the Six Pillars into action to help them solve the issue of racism in the Locker Room. Coach Smitty decides the first step is to apologize to Marcellus and the second step is to have a frank and open discussion with all the players. It is this locker room discussion that will decide Davey's future.

Deep Dive Teaching

Think about how a coffee bean affects boiling water. It turns it into coffee, right? You take a negative or difficult situation (the boiling water) and with the power of that little bean giving of its positive effort, change happens. It turns the bad situation into a good opportunity.

We want to be like the coffee bean in this metaphor: a positive presence giving of ourselves in service of beneficial change. No matter what your circumstances are or what you are going through right now, there is an opportunity to effect change— even if that change at first is only to your own attitude.

Just as a coffee bean improves the boiling water by turning it into coffee, you can change a difficult situation for the better. You just have to be willing to stay positive, serve others, and remain humble. Let's look at the three keys that will help us to be coffee beans: Positivity, Service, and Humility.

Positivity. You will either infect others or affect others. When you smile and have positive body language, others will smile and be positive with you. The opposite is also true; when you scowl and have negative body language, others are going to treat you in the same manner. Being positive isn't the same as being soft. In fact, it's really tough to stay positive when you're in a difficult situation or things aren't going your way.

Service. A coffee bean doesn't bully the water into becoming coffee. It gives of itself to make a change. Service to others is at the heart of creating change. It is only by asking what you can do for others that you see the way forward to make things better for everyone.

Humility. This may be the most important part of being a coffee bean: it requires humility. Being positive when others around you are negative or even threatening requires humility. Serving others before yourself requires humility. Working to create change for the betterment of everyone requires humility. It's the basis of the whole thing.

For the Individual

My Key Takeaways

1. _____

2. _____

3. _____

Journal Questions

1. In a difficult situation that you are facing, how can you be a coffee bean?
2. Why is it important not to under- or over-apologize?
3. What are some signs that an apology or act of repentance is proportional to the mistake you made?
4. What standard do you hold yourself to?
5. Overcoming adversity requires that you focus on where you want to finish. What end point are you focusing on to help you overcome current (or recent) adversity?

Exercise

Coffee Bean Commitments

This exercise will help you think about the ways that you can be a positive influence on your family, friends, and community.

- **Step 1**: *Word Association*. Set a timer for seven minutes. Using the list of words and phrases following, write down as many things as come to mind related to the prompts. Don't worry about using complete sentences or phrasing things properly, and keep in mind that you can draw instead of writing if you're more prone to doodling.
- **Step 2**: *Brainstorming*. Set the timer for an additional 10 minutes. Use the following list to brainstorm ways that you can contribute in a positive way to your friends, family, and community. Make notes as you go. Ask questions like:
  - How does this word relate to my skills or talents?
  - How does this phrase relate to a need that my friends or family have?
  - What does this word make me think of in relation to my community?

- **Step 3**: *Commitments*. Don't set a timer for this one; just let it take however long it takes. With your word association and brainstorming notes, identify five things that will help you be a positive influence on your family, friends, and community. Write these down as "I will" statements. For example:
  - I will pause to take a breath, so I can think before I speak.
  - I will look for an opportunity to help a friend, family member, or neighbor every single day.
  - I will notice negative thoughts and restructure them in a positive way.

Prompts

Humility

Service

Positivity

Negativity

Black and white

Necessary

Fun

Charity

Love

Food and drink

For the Team

Discussion Questions

1. What adversity is your team currently facing? This could be an external or internal obstacle to your team's success.
2. Where do you need to focus so that you can finish on the other side of that obstacle?
3. How can your team be like a coffee bean?
4. What is your team standard? Is anyone above it?
5. What is your team's standard for apologies or atonement for mistakes?

Exercise

Overcoming Obstacles

The goal of this exercise is for team members to communicate, to trust each other, and to overcome obstacles together.

- Set up obstacles over a large space, like a basketball court or half a football field or an empty parking lot. Obstacles can be stacks of cones, pyramids of cardboard boxes, chairs, bikes, bowling pins, rolled up sleeping bags, and so on. Really, anything can be an obstacle. These don't need to be placed particularly strategically; just random placement is fine.

- Separate team members into groups of two to four people each, depending on how difficult you want things to be. Partners will be easier, while a group of four will require greater communication skills.
- Teams will take turns trying to navigate the obstacle course while blindfolded in the least amount of time.
  - *Teams of Two*: One person navigates the course with a blindfold while the other person directs them from the finish line.
  - *Teams of Three*: One person navigates the course with a blindfold while the other two people direct them from the finish line.
  - *Teams of Four*: Two people navigate the course blindfolded while the other two people direct them from the finish line.

The team that makes it through the course in the fastest time (and with the least amount of upset to the obstacles) wins.

Notes

11

Vulnerability Is a Strength

For Everyone

Core Lessons

- Apologies must be authentic and sincere, with no expectation that the apology will be accepted.
- Apologies can give closure and validation, as well as relieving guilt and shame.
- Apologies make you vulnerable, but vulnerability is a strength.

Chapter Summary

Coach Smitty meets with Marcellus one-on-one in his office so he can offer a heartfelt apology for his behavior that morning. Marcellus has many competing emotions regarding the apology, and he only partially accepts it. But Coach Smitty knows that an apology must be given without any expectation of acceptance by the wounded party. Together they walk out to talk to the rest of the team about the broken locker room.

Deep Dive Teaching

Apologizing when you've hurt someone is not an easy thing to do. It puts you in a vulnerable position because there's always the chance that they won't accept the apology. But an apology is worthwhile because it can bring peace and validation to the person receiving the apology, and it can be a vehicle to relieve guilt and shame for the person making the apology.

There are three key pieces to making an apology. Let's look at each briefly.

Acknowledge what you did wrong. The first step to apologizing for hurting someone is to simply acknowledge how your actions hurt them. Own the mistake. Don't try to make excuses for why you did what you did. Even if you had very good reasons, the fact is that the other person was harmed by something you did or said. Acknowledge that completely.

Be sincere. It's pretty clear when someone is only apologizing because they feel that they have to do so. Don't apologize out of a sense of duty. Instead, approach it from a place of genuine desire to make amends.

Leave the ball in their court. You may owe the other person an apology, but they don't owe you anything in return. Don't try to finangle an acceptance of the apology from them. It's entirely possible that an apology alone is not sufficient for forgiveness. It's a great starting point, though.

Apologies make you vulnerable, but never forget: vulnerability is a strength.

For the Individual

My Key Takeaways

1. _____

2. _____

3. _____

Journal Questions

1. Who is someone that you should have apologized to but didn't?
2. How does not making that apology continue to affect you?
3. Who is someone that you think should apologize to you?
4. How would that apology have to be delivered for you to accept it and forgive?
5. What makes apologizing difficult?

Exercise

Write the Script

- Prepare for a needed apology by writing a script to guide you through the interaction.
- First, write down what you did and why you did it.

- Second, write down what you will say to the other person (excluding the Why because that would be making excuses).
- Third, write down possible responses the other person could give from accepting the apology immediately to expressing continued hurt to rejecting the apology outright.
- Finally, write down how you could respond constructively to each of the possible responses from the third step.

For the Team

Discussion Questions

1. What are some signs that an apology is sincere?
2. How would you respond if someone didn't accept your apology?
3. If you don't know what you did to upset someone, how can you find out?
4. What are some benefits to apologizing when you've wronged someone (other than those mentioned in the teaching)?
5. How is vulnerability a strength?

Exercise

I Apologize

- Divide the group into pairs to practice apologies. Each partner should practice both roles: giving and receiving the apology. Switch pairs periodically so everyone works with multiple people.

- The list following provides some ideas for the person apologizing to role play.
- The person receiving the apology can either accept, reject, or counter the apology.
  - Accept: The person will forgive the other with the apology alone.
  - Reject: The person will not accept the apology or forgive.
  - Counter: The person will accept the apology but forgiveness will be contingent on other conditions.

Role Play Ideas

You excluded the other person from a group gathering that they should have been invited to.

You called them lazy and worthless when you thought they couldn't hear you.

You started dating your friend's ex less than a week after they broke up.

You stole the spotlight from the other person when they should have been the main focus.

You said you would help them over the weekend but then you bailed to go play golf instead.

You cut them off in traffic and caused an accident.

You borrowed a book and then lost it.

You insulted their family.

You made plans for the evening but then decided to hang out with someone else instead.

You dismissed their ideas in a derogatory way in front of other people.

Notes

_____

_____

_____

_____

_____

_____

_____

_____

_____

_____

_____

_____

_____

_____

_____

_____

_____

_____

_____

_____

_____

_____

_____

_____

_____

_____

_____

_____

_____

_____

_____

_____

_____

_____

_____

_____

_____

_____

_____

_____

_____

12

Team Meeting

For Everyone

Core Lessons

- Leaders step up to do what is right even when they're scared.
- Everyone deserves to have their voice heard, even if you disagree with what they have to say.

Chapter Summary

Coach Smitty informs the team that they will be "practicing" in the locker room. He goes on to say that he mishandled the Davey situation, and he apologizes to the team. He also apologizes to Coach Washington for ignoring his advice to handle the matter openly. He reiterates his apology to Marcellus so the entire team knows that he recognizes he treated him badly. The football becomes a microphone for everyone to have their turn to speak so that the team can begin to heal the hurts of the broken locker room.

Deep Dive Teaching

At its simplest, integrity is calling right, right and wrong, wrong.

At the beginning of this story, Marcellus did what Coach Smitty had trained his team to do: he saw wrong and he called it out. But Coach Smitty was not able to accept that at the time. Over the course of the story, Coach Smitty comes to see the error he made. He did not act with the same integrity that Marcellus showed. But in this chapter he has seen the error and is, himself, using his integrity to call wrong, wrong.

It's not easy to call out others when they are wrong. It's not easy to be the only one standing up saying "This is not right," when everyone else is just going with the flow. When push comes to shove, it's not easy to demonstrate integrity.

And sometimes, as happened to Marcellus, others will shut us down when we call right, right or wrong, wrong. But integrity demands that we speak up regardless of how the message is received. If others shut you down when your integrity has you speaking the truth, don't be discouraged. Don't let that silencing be the end of the story.

It's scary to behave with integrity. It's scary to speak up when everyone else is shutting up. And it's scary to admit when you have been wrong. There's nothing wrong with being scared. But there is something wrong with not finding the courage to press forward anyway.

Right is right and wrong is wrong. Integrity knows the difference and speaks up about it.

For the Individual

My Key Takeaways

1. _____

2. _____

3. _____

Journal Questions

1. What does integrity mean to you?
2. What's an example of a time when you acted with integrity?
3. What about an example of a time when you did not act with integrity?
4. How did you know that right was right and wrong was wrong in these situations?
5. What led you to act the way that you did?

Exercise

Mindful Meditation

- Set a timer for 5 to 10 minutes.
- Find a place to sit comfortably, either in a chair or on the floor. Place one hand over your heart and the other over your gut.

- Take a few slow, deep breaths and try to settle into your skin.
- Let your breath even out to a natural rhythm and just sit until the timer goes off.

  Okay, don't just sit. Here are six things you can do while you're sitting there:
  1. Listen to the sounds of the room or the world outside.
  2. Listen to your breathing.
  3. Feel your heartbeat.
  4. Feel your gut and what's going on inside.
  5. Notice which thoughts try to steal your attention.
  6. Notice the way those thoughts affect your heart and your gut.

For the Team

Discussion Questions

1. Why is integrity an important character trait for your team?
2. How does your integrity impact your contribution to the team?
3. What are some rules that would be useful for a potentially heated team discussion?
4. Why is it important to listen to your teammates' thoughts and feelings, even if you disagree with them?

5. What is the elephant in the room that your team needs to discuss?

Exercise

Two Facts and a Lie

- Each team member writes down two things that are true and one thing that is a lie.
- Traditionally, this team-building game is played as a "getting-to-know-you" exercise, and players write down personal facts for their truths and lies. In this case, the goal is to open up further discussion about integrity; therefore, players will instead write down two general facts that they know to be true and one that they know to be false.
- Players will take turns reading their three facts. The other players can then ask up to three questions to get clues that point to which is the false statement. The player reading the facts does not have to answer these questions truthfully. In other words, they can try to come up with convincing lies to get people to guess incorrectly.
- On sheets of paper, players will write down which statement they think is the false one beside each person's name.
- For each false statement they identify, players get one point. In addition, players get one point

for each person who incorrectly identifies one of their truths as a lie. The winner is the person with the most points.

- Follow up this exercise with a discussion about what it felt like to lie, how they could tell others were lying or telling the truth, and why truth and integrity matter.

Notes

13

Humility and Grace

For Everyone

Core Lessons

- When a person comes to you wanting to learn and willing to listen with humility, then it's your responsibility to respond to and teach that person with grace.
- Words are powerful. Once spoken, they can never be unsaid. Choose your words wisely.

Chapter Summary

Coach Washington begins the discussion at the team meeting because he knows it is important for the minority athletes to hear from someone who looks like them. He encourages the team to treat each other with humility and grace as they take this opportunity to hear and be heard. The team meeting is long and intense, but the athletes treat each other with respect throughout. After listening to all of his teammates speak, Davey takes the ball for his turn.

Deep Dive Teaching

Toughness isn't just about being able to take a hit on the field or to bounce back from a rejection. Toughness is also about being able to stand still in the face of tension and discomfort. Toughness is about digging deep and doing what needs to be done.

In this chapter, the team gathers for an uncomfortable and tense conversation about racism. Perhaps racism isn't your team's problem. Maybe your team struggles with hazing or bullying. Maybe your team struggles to attract players who are dedicated to the team. Maybe your team struggles with drug use or underage drinking.

The list of potential problems could go on, but the first step to solving them all is the same: talk about it. Problems thrive in the dark, like mold in the leftovers that got pushed to the back of the fridge. Talking about these issues openly, with grace and humility, is the first step to finding a solution.

Make no mistake, the discussion will not be easy. There will be people in the group who aren't on the same page. There will be dissent. There will be continuing undercurrents of conflict. One deep conversation, no matter how good, will not solve whatever serious issues your team faces. But it's a great start.

It is tough to have a discussion like this. It's tough to sit still and listen to others discuss uncomfortable issues. It's tough to sit still and give your honest viewpoint on a difficult topic. But you are tough enough to overcome. You are tough enough to dig deep and do what needs to be done.

For the Individual

My Key Takeaways

1. _____

2. _____

3. _____

Journal Questions

1. What is a difficult topic that you wish your team would have a discussion about?
2. Why is that topic important to you?
3. What would you say during your turn to speak in such a discussion?
4. How can you remind yourself to listen to others' viewpoints with humility and grace?
5. Give an example of a time when you did not choose your words carefully. What happened as a result?

Exercise

Rant and Rave

- Think about that difficult topic that you selected in the journal questions, or pick another topic that you have strong opinions about or want discussed by your team.
- Set a timer for three minutes.
  - Have a nice long rant to an empty room about this topic until the timer goes off. Say whatever comes to mind. Imagine opponents being rude or dismissive of what you're saying. Have a shouting match with the air, pace around, wave your fists. Get emphatic.
- Set a timer for three more minutes.
  - Write down what you said and felt (as well as you remember) along with anything you left out during the three minute verbal rant. Write until the timer goes off.
- Take 10 slow, deep breaths, pausing between each inhale and exhale.
- Set a timer for three minutes again.
  - In these three minutes, write down a calmer, more rational and clearer-headed version of what you wanted to say about the topic. Honor your feelings and include them in your writing, but choose your words carefully this time.

For the Team

Discussion Questions

1. What is a difficult topic that your team needs to discuss?
2. Can your team have that discussion with humility and grace? Why or why not?
3. How does toughness help you to have humility and grace in a difficult conversation?
4. Why is it important to talk about difficult topics instead of avoiding them?
5. How do humility and grace help you to be a better team?

Exercise

Who's Going to Win the Super Bowl?   With this exercise, you'll practice having difficult discussions with humility and grace.

- The team members will each need to pick a side on an issue that isn't very important but still gets people excited and potentially overly enthusiastic.
  - For example, who's going to win the Super Bowl? Or the NBA Playoffs? Which country is going to take the most medals in the next Olympic games? Who's going to win the next FIFA World Cup? Which superhero movie is the best? What video game is the most fun?

- Have team members take turns speaking as they pass a football to signal whose turn it is to speak. The team member with the ball (or whatever object is being used) has 30 seconds to say whatever they want about the topic, but it has to be relevant and they must remain respectful of their teammates.
- Try to have at least one or two "plants" in the group who will play devil's advocate to get people riled up a little.
- After everyone has had a turn to speak, discuss how things went. How respectful were people of each other and of differing opinions? How could there have been more humility or grace?

Notes

_____

_____

_____

_____

_____

_____

_____

_____

_____

_____

_____

_____

_____

_____

_____

_____

_____

_____

_____

_____

_____

_____

_____

_____

_____

_____

_____

_____

_____

_____

_____

_____

_____

_____

_____

_____

_____

_____

_____

_____

_____

_____

_____

14

I Want the Ball

For Everyone

Core Lessons

- Making a mistake doesn't make YOU a mistake.
- Forgiveness doesn't heal the hurt, but it's a good place to start.

Chapter Summary

Davey and Marcellus are the last two athletes to speak after a long and intense sharing session with the whole team. Davey has finally seen the error of what he said at the party, as well as how he handled things afterward. From a place of understanding, he accepts responsibility for his actions and prepares himself to face the consequences. Marcellus speaks last, expressing forgiveness to both Coach Smitty and Davey, even going so far as to offer to run Davey's punishment miles with him. The hurt and the trials are not over, but the team has taken a giant step toward overcoming them.

Deep Dive Teaching

When someone hurts us, we feel varied emotions. We might be angry, hurt, or betrayed. We might want to hurt them like they've hurt us. We might be ready to write them off and never speak to them again. Pain and its accompanying emotions can lead us in a lot of different directions, but there is only one path that brings about healing: forgiveness.

Forgiveness does not instantly heal the hurt, but it's the only place to start. Think of it in terms of a physical wound. If you get a deep cut, a simple bandage or ignoring the cut isn't going to heal the wound. You need to get stitches. Stitches are uncomfortable, and they aren't magic. But they will lead to healing over time so that you might not even see a scar by the end.

Forgiveness is a lot like stitches. It's uncomfortable. It doesn't magically fix everything. But it helps to heal emotional wounds over time. Let's look at three steps that can help you forgive someone who has hurt you.

1. *Look at it from their perspective.* Try to understand why they did what they did. Give them a chance to explain. It will be easy to dismiss what they say as just excuses, but fight that urge. Try to give them the benefit of the doubt.

2. *Meditate or pray.* Whether you believe in a higher power or not, sitting quietly in contemplation of what has happened can help you reach a place of forgiveness. This isn't about sitting around ranting to yourself about the injustice. It's about letting yourself feel what you feel and then moving that along, out of your system.

3. *Reverse the roles.* In your head, imagine what you would want to happen if, instead, you were the one who had done the hurting. How would you want them to treat you afterward? Would you want them to offer you forgiveness?

Forgiveness is not an instant cure or a magic elixir. It's a step in the right direction on the path to healing.

For the Individual

My Key Takeaways

1. _____

2. _____

3. _____

Journal Questions

1. What makes forgiveness so hard to give and receive?
2. When you make a mistake, do *you* feel like a mistake? Why or why not?
3. Who is someone that you trusted but who has hurt you?
4. What would it take for you to forgive that person?
5. How do grace and humility play into forgiveness?

Exercise

A New Perspective

- Grab your phone (or an actual camera) and take a picture of one wall of your bedroom. It doesn't matter which wall: just pick one.
- Now sit down and take a picture of the same wall, both straight on and looking up.
- Lay down and do the same thing.
- Find a step stool or sturdy chair to stand on to do the same.
- Move to a corner of the room and take another picture. Then, go to the opposite corner.
- Now that you have all of these pictures, compare them.
  - What can you see in one picture that you can't see in another?
  - What different perceptions of you might people get from the different perspectives of the pictures?
  - How does the change of perspective alter how you see the room?

For the Team

Discussion Questions

1. How does forgiveness help to heal hurt over time?
2. How can you gain new or different perspectives on an issue?
3. What helps your teammates to come together to forgive each other?
4. How does forgiveness benefit both the person giving it and the person receiving it?
5. What are some of the next steps to heal hurts after forgiveness has been given?

Exercise

Role Reversal

- Pair up the team members with people they don't spend much time with. Break up any cliques there might be for this exercise.
- The amount of time this goes on can vary from 30 minutes to an entire day. For the first half of the time, Person 1 will try to do Person 2's job. Person 1 can only give them advice during the first 5 to 10 minutes of this; after that, they just watch. For the second half, the roles switch and Person 2 will try to do Person 1's job.

- Discussion after this exercise should focus on the following:
  - What insight did you gain into the other person's role on the team?
  - What didn't you know before doing this? Or what did you learn?
  - What insight did you gain into your own position or role on the team from seeing someone else perform that role?
  - How do these different perspectives help you to see others in a new way?

Notes

_____

_____

_____

_____

_____

_____

_____

_____

_____

_____

_____

_____

_____

_____

_____

_____

_____

_____

_____

_____

_____

_____

_____

_____

_____

_____

_____

_____

_____

_____

_____

_____

_____

_____

_____

_____

_____

_____

_____

_____

_____

_____

_____